SNAPSHOTS IN HISTORY

THE PROGRESSIVE PARTY

The Success of a Failed Party

by Hilarie Staton

JAN 2008

THE PROGRESSIVE PARTY

The Success of a Failed Party

by Hilarie Staton

Content Adviser: Tom Lansford, Ph.D., Assistant Dean
and Associate Professor of Political Science,
College of Arts and Letters, University of Southern Mississippi

Reading Adviser: Katie Van Sluys, Ph.D.,
School of Education, DePaul University

Compass Point Books ◆ Minneapolis, Minnesota

COMPASS POINT BOOKS

3109 West 50th Street, #115
Minneapolis, MN 55410

Visit Compass Point Books on the Internet at
www.compasspointbooks.com
or e-mail your request to
custserv@compasspointbooks.com

For Compass Point Books
Jennifer VanVoorst, Jaime Martens, XNR Productions, Inc.,
Catherine Neitge, Keith Griffin, and Carol Jones

Produced by White-Thomson Publishing Ltd.

For White-Thomson Publishing
Stephen White-Thomson, Susan Crean, Amy Sparks,
Tinstar Design Ltd., Tom Lansford, Peggy Bresnick Kendler,
Will Hare, and Timothy Griffin

Library of Congress Cataloging-in-Publication Data
Staton, Hilarie.
  The Progressive Party : the success of a failed party / by Hilarie
Staton.
      p. cm. — (Snapshots in history)
  Includes bibliographical references and index.
  ISBN-13: 978-0-7565-2451-7 (library binding)
  ISBN-10: 0-7565-2451-2 (library binding)
  ISBN-13: 978-0-7565-3170-6 (paperback)
  ISBN-10: 0-7565-3170-5 (paperback)
1. Progressive Party (1912)—Juvenile literature. 2. Progressivism
(United States politics)—Juvenile literature. 3. United States—Politics
and government—1909–1913—Juvenile literature. 4. United
States—Politics and government—1913–1921—Juvenile literature. I.
Title. II. Series.
  JK2387.S83 2006
  324.2732'7—dc22   2006027081

CONTENTS

The Republican Party Splits

Republicans from all over the country began arriving in Chicago in early June for the 1912 Republican National Convention. The convention would not begin until June 18, but powerful Republicans were already meeting. In a highly unusual move, former President Theodore Roosevelt, who was one of the people in the race to become the Republican Party's candidate for president, also came to Chicago early. In those days, the nominees to be a party's candidate did not go to the national convention.

Cries of "Teddy! Teddy! We want Teddy!" greeted Roosevelt as he and his family made their way to their hotel on Saturday, June 15. The police held back the mob of supporters so the Roosevelts could enter the hotel.

During the Republican National Convention, the Republican Party contained two different groups. Roosevelt was the leader of the progressives, a group that supported ideas different from those of the main Republican Party. Roosevelt was not happy with how the government had been run since he left office in 1909. He and other progressives believed that President William Howard Taft had broken his promise to continue Roosevelt's policies of regulating big business, reforming government, and fighting against corruption.

Former President Theodore Roosevelt was a popular figure among progressive Republicans.

NATIONAL CONVENTIONS

Both the Democrats and Republicans, the two main political parties in the United States, hold national conventions every four years. At the conventions, delegates from each state select their party's candidates to run for president and vice president. The leaders of the party present a platform, which states the party's positions on key issues. Conventions are often celebrations and times of great optimism, but the 1912 Republican National Convention in Chicago was more about differences within the party.

On the other side, conservative Republicans— including most of the Republican Party leaders— supported Taft as their candidate. Conservatives wanted to limit the government's role in regulating businesses. They were not interested in changing the way the government was run.

In the days leading up to the convention, Roosevelt held secret meetings with progressive Republican leaders to plan a strategy to become the Republican candidate for president. Rumors about a split within the Republican Party started to spread.

But despite his efforts and his popularity, Roosevelt still had to contend with a delegate-selection process that was wide open to corruption. In most states, political leaders selected the delegates who would represent their state at the national convention. Most of these leaders were conservative Republicans who supported Taft. However, in 1912, for the first time in U.S. history,

By the 1912 Republican Convention, President Taft (right) had become much more conservative, which caused a split with his old friend, progressive Teddy Roosevelt.

12 states held presidential state primary elections. In a presidential primary, voters directly decide whom they want their state delegates to support at a political party's national convention. Roosevelt had won nine of the 12 primaries and gained 278 delegates in the primary elections, compared with only 48 delegates for Taft.

But Taft claimed an additional 557 delegates from the states without a primary—enough to make him the Republican candidate. Roosevelt did not agree with Taft's count and accused him of replacing Roosevelt delegates with Taft delegates to win the nomination.

The Republican National Committee, which runs the party, met to decide who would get the disputed delegates. They allowed Roosevelt only 19 of the 254 disputed delegates, which meant that Taft still had enough delegates to become the Republican candidate for president. Roosevelt was angry but not surprised, and he was certainly not ready to give up his bid for the presidency. Roosevelt told his advisers:

> *I went before the people and I won. Now the national committee and a portion of the convention, which is made a majority only by the aid of delegates not elected but chosen by the national committee, are trying to cheat me out of the nomination. They can't do it.*

On Monday, June 17, Roosevelt spoke to 6,000 progressive supporters at an auditorium in Chicago. Thousands more lined the streets outside just to see him as he entered and left the auditorium. They sang patriotic songs and cheered for their hero. Roosevelt gave a passionate speech about the aims of progressive Republicans. He said:

> *Friends, here in Chicago at this time you have a great task before you. I wish you to realize deep in your hearts that you are not merely facing a crisis in the history of a party. You are facing a crisis in the history of a nation. ... We fight in honorable fashion for the good of mankind; fearless of the future; unheeding of our individual fates; with unflinching hearts and undimmed eyes.*

The next day, despite the rift between the conservatives and progressives, the Republican National Convention officially began. A thousand police officers were there to prevent trouble, and they broke up countless fistfights among Republicans. Writer Edna Ferber was reporting from the convention for the *Emporia Gazette* newspaper and later recalled that there was "never for one minute anything but a mass of screaming, shouting, stamping, hooting maniacs."

Throughout the convention, heated debates and discussions about delegates and the process of

The Republican Convention of 1912 was torn apart by bitter arguments among delegates.

13

selecting delegates took place. Roosevelt continued to challenge Taft and his supporters, since he believed that he was the clear winner and should receive the party's nomination.

On Saturday, June 22, all Republican delegates—both progressive and conservative—came to the convention hall. Although they already knew how many votes each nominee had, they had to officially choose the Republican candidates for president and vice president. Warren G. Harding, an Ohio conservative who had just lost a race for governor, nominated Taft as the Republican candidate. Kansas newspaperman Henry J. Allen responded to Taft's nomination by reading a message from Theodore Roosevelt:

> *Under the direction, and with the encouragement of Mr. Taft, the majority of the National Committee ... stole 80 or 90 delegates ... a sufficient number of fraudulent delegates to defeat the fully expressed will of the people and to substitute a dishonest for an honest majority. ... The men elected as Roosevelt delegates will now decline to vote on any matter before the convention.*

As Roosevelt promised, most of his delegates sat silent as the voting began. They did not vote. The final count gave Taft 561 votes, more than enough to become the Republican candidate for president. After the vote, Roosevelt's delegates walked out of the convention in protest.

That night, Roosevelt spoke to his progressive supporters at a nearby auditorium. Thousands came to hear him, and thousands more crowded the streets to see him. The crowd yelled, "We want Teddy!" Roosevelt called his followers to action:

> *I, therefore, ask you to go to your ... homes to find out the sentiment of the people ... and then again come together, I suggest by mass convention, to nominate a progressive on a progressive platform that will enable us to appeal to Northerner and Southerner, Easterner and Westerner, Republican and Democrat alike in the name of our common American citizenship. If you wish me to make the fight, I will make it.*

Loud cheers greeted Roosevelt's speech. The former president was not only calling for the formation of a new political party, but he was also volunteering to be its candidate for president.

The new party would represent what many American voters wanted: a government that worked to improve life for everyone, not just the rich owners of big business. It would be called the Progressive Party.

THE BULL MOOSE

During the Republican National Convention, a reporter called out to Roosevelt and asked how he felt. "I'm as fit as a bull moose," Roosevelt answered. That remark earned Roosevelt the nickname "Bull Moose." The new Progressive Party was called the Bull Moose Party, and Roosevelt's vice-presidential candidate, Hiram Johnson, was called the Vice Moose.

15

The Muckrakers

Chapter

2

At the time Roosevelt formed the Progressive Party, the progressive movement itself was already more than 30 years old. In fact, the years from 1880 to 1920 are often referred to as the Progressive Era. During this time, reform-minded Americans exposed a variety of problems, such as unhealthful city slums and dangerous factory conditions. These reformers were called progressives because they wanted the United States to progress, or move forward, to become a better place. Among other things, progressives wanted the American government to better serve the poor and working classes.

Reform was necessary because the country itself had changed. For the first 100 years of its history, the United States was a rural society, with most of its economy based on farming. By the 1880s, however, it had become an industrial, urban society with factories, large businesses, and overcrowded cities. Some cities had grown so fast that poor families were packed into tiny apartments or homes without fresh water, sunlight, or bathrooms. Many American men, women, and children took jobs in factories and mines where they worked in unhealthful and dangerous conditions for long hours and low pay.

In cities like New York, poor families lived in small, dark, crowded apartments.

Progressives wanted the government to take an active role in changing American society, but they did not always agree on which problems needed attention. Some progressives thought that one problem, such as the growth of big business, was the root cause of many others. Some blamed alcohol for many social problems and favored prohibition, or outlawing the sale of alcoholic drinks, to bring about reform. Other progressives thought that the government's focus should be on educating the poor so they could live a better life.

Author and photographer Jacob Riis introduced many Americans to the horrors of being a poor immigrant in the city. In his 1890 book, *How the Other Half Lives*, Riis described conditions in New York City slum apartments:

Through his writing, Jacob Riis exposed the conditions in which poor people lived.

> *The hall is dark and you might stumble over children. ... All the fresh air that ever enters these stairs comes from the hall-door that is forever slamming. ... That was a woman filling her pail by the hydrant you just bumped against. The sinks are in the hallway, that all the tenants may have access—and all be poisoned alike by the summer stenches.*

Riis was known as a muckraker, a person who searches out and exposes problems in society. Many muckrakers were writers or journalists who wanted to shock readers into taking action. During the Progressive Era, muckrakers exposed unhealthful urban living conditions, dangerous factories, and unhealthful food. Muckrakers also examined the links businesses had with the government.

As industry became more important to the economy of the country, businesses increasingly controlled the lives of many Americans. Businesses that wanted to keep their costs down and profits up often did so at the expense of workers. If employees

RAKING MUCK

Future Progressive Party candidate Theodore Roosevelt was the first to use the term *muckraker*. In a speech on April 14, 1906, Roosevelt, then president, compared the journalists who were exposing corruption in government and harsh working conditions to muckrakers—people who raked manure and filth with a special rake called a muck rake. Roosevelt believed that these writers were going too far. In time, though, the muckrakers would convince Roosevelt and other progressives that reform was necessary.

19

worked long hours for low pay, for example, the businesses made bigger profits. Some companies also looked to the government to help them make profits. By influencing corrupt politicians, businesses could be favored in bids for government work or could influence government regulations regarding working conditions, pollution, and pay.

Political bosses ran many city and state governments. They helped officials get elected and then demanded big favors in return. They bribed politicians at all levels of government. In California, for example, powerful railroad companies bribed politicians to ensure that no laws were passed to control them. These companies charged high prices and paid low wages. Their owners got very rich. In a series of articles called "Shame of the Cities," reporter Lincoln Steffens described the corrupt city governments in St. Louis,

THE TRIANGLE FACTORY FIRE

Sometimes tragic events, such as the 1911 fire at the Triangle Shirtwaist Factory in New York City, exposed horrible factory conditions. Nearly 150 young female factory workers died in the fire. An investigation into the fire revealed that the workers' tables were too close together and that there were no fire extinguishers. Even worse, the doors of the factory had been locked; therefore, the women could not escape the fire. News of this harrowing event shocked middle-class Americans. It spurred many Americans to join the progressive movement that was pressuring the government to regulate the working conditions in factories.

Philadelphia, and Chicago, among others. He wrote that politicians were being paid by big businesses and that they were buying votes and using political bosses.

At the time, companies were largely unregulated and were seemingly free to behave however they pleased. Many well-known American companies, such as the Standard Oil Co., were exposed as having corrupt business practices. They formed trusts, groups of companies that worked together to control industries. In her book *The History of Standard Oil Company*, reporter Ida Tarbell described how John D. Rockefeller had organized the oil trust, which in turn put other companies out of business and controlled the price of oil. Because of the trust's monopoly of the oil industry, Americans were paying a high price for oil. Trusts in other industries, such as the railroads, were hurting Americans in similar ways.

By 1900, many Americans realized they were needlessly paying a high price for their modern, urban, industrial world. Goods were more expensive because big businesses controlled whole industries. Their government was run by corrupt men who were paid by these big businesses. Progressives did not feel it was hopeless, though. They believed that if they worked together, these problems could be solved. ◣

A Movement For Change

Chapter

3

During the Progressive Era, Americans took notice of the problems the muckrakers exposed, and they tried to solve them. Some reformers banded together to make changes.

Labor unions, for example, tried to bring about change in the workplace. Union leaders organized mine workers, railroad workers, garment workers, and workers from many other important industries. Unions fought for better pay and improved working conditions, often by holding strikes or protests. Their strikes often turned violent, though, and the government usually supported the businesses that the unions challenged. The workers in most industries had no one to help them until the progressive movement began to take notice.

Many of those who took part in the progressive movement were well-educated, middle-class professionals in their 20s and 30s who had moved from rural areas to cities to find work. These doctors, teachers, lawyers, and social workers were exposed to the awful conditions in which poor urban workers lived. They became progressives because they believed Americans and the government could improve the lives of these people. As the movement grew, some African-Americans and labor leaders joined as well.

Soon millions of Americans felt the progressive movement represented their political views. They

Union strikes often turned violent when the military became involved.

23

wanted the government to regulate business practices and expose corrupt politicians. They wanted their government and business leaders to make decisions that were morally right, rather than making decisions for profit. Other Americans, however, held conservative beliefs and did not seem to be as concerned about the problems the growing country was facing. They believed that conditions would eventually improve by themselves, without help from reformers or the government.

In the late 1800s, social workers began to tackle some of the problems facing poor people living in American cities. At that time, many college-educated, middle-class women chose to become social workers. The most famous of these was Jane Addams, who studied the problems of the poor, especially women and children. In 1889, she opened Hull House in a poor Chicago neighborhood. Hull House was a settlement house, a facility that helped local residents by providing community services such as adult education and health care. At Hull House, people could get health services and take courses in reading and writing. More settlement houses opened in other cities, but only a handful of the millions of poor people living in American cities were helped by them.

When Addams saw that reform was not happening quickly enough, she took matters into her own hands. Hilda Satt Polacheck, who attended classes at Hull House and later taught there, described Addams' efforts:

Jane Addams and other middle-class social workers used their education to improve the lives of the poor.

Bad housing of the thousands of immigrants who lived near Hull House was the concern of Jane Addams. ... Alleys were filled with large wooden boxes where garbage and horse manure were dumped. In most cases these boxes did not have covers and were breeding places for flies and rats. ... Jane Addams was told that the city ... could do nothing else. When the time came to renew contracts for garbage collection, Miss Addams ... put in her bid to collect garbage. Her bid was never considered, but she was appointed garbage inspector.

Child labor was of concern to the progressives. In the late 1800s, many children in the United States worked in various industries. They were paid very little for long hours of dangerous work, including crawling under machines or into mines. Their families were poor and desperately needed the money they earned. But working children could not attend school, and so with no way to receive an education, the cycle of poverty continued.

Another issue of the Progressive Era was women's suffrage. Women did many things to make the country a better place, but they had no say in the laws that affected them. They wanted the right to vote so they could be full participants in American society and choose the leaders who make and enforce laws.

Children were hired to do dangerous work in factories and mines because their quickness and small size allowed them to do jobs that adults could not.

THE END OF CHILD LABOR

Progressives eventually helped put an end to child labor by helping to pass laws that required children to attend school until a certain age. In 1916, Congress passed the Keating-Owen Act to stop child labor completely. However, the Supreme Court found the law unconstitutional because it affected trade between states. All states had passed laws opposing child labor by 1918. It was not until the 1938 Fair Labor Standards Act that the federal government made child labor illegal.

In 1869, the Wyoming Territory had granted women the right to vote. When Wyoming became a state in 1890, it became the first state where women could vote since the early days of the country. Other Western states followed suit, but it would take nearly 30 years before all women had the right to vote.

Yet another reform movement that grew during the Progressive Era was the temperance movement. For years, its members, which included both progressives and conservatives, had worked to pass laws to control the sale and use of alcoholic beverages. Supporters of this movement believed that most problems of the poor happened because people drank too much alcohol. In the late 1800s, several states passed laws to control the sale of liquor. However, since these laws were not enforced, some reformers took action.

Activist Carry Nation joined the temperance movement partly because of experiences in her

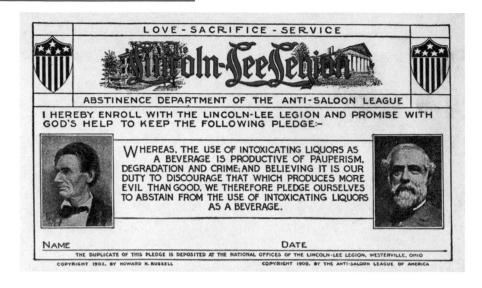

LOVE - SACRIFICE - SERVICE

Lincoln-Lee Legion

ABSTINENCE DEPARTMENT OF THE ANTI-SALOON LEAGUE

I HEREBY ENROLL WITH THE LINCOLN-LEE LEGION AND PROMISE WITH GOD'S HELP TO KEEP THE FOLLOWING PLEDGE:-

WHEREAS, THE USE OF INTOXICATING LIQUORS AS A BEVERAGE IS PRODUCTIVE OF PAUPERISM, DEGRADATION AND CRIME; AND BELIEVING IT IS OUR DUTY TO DISCOURAGE THAT WHICH PRODUCES MORE EVIL THAN GOOD, WE THEREFORE PLEDGE OURSELVES TO ABSTAIN FROM THE USE OF INTOXICATING LIQUORS AS A BEVERAGE.

NAME   DATE

THE DUPLICATE OF THIS PLEDGE IS DEPOSITED AT THE NATIONAL OFFICES OF THE LINCOLN-LEE LEGION, WESTERVILLE, OHIO

COPYRIGHT 1903, BY HOWARD H. RUSSELL   COPYRIGHT 1909, BY THE ANTI-SALOON LEAGUE OF AMERICA

Members of the temperance movement took an oath that they would abstain from drinking alcohol.

own life. Her first husband had died of alcoholism, so she knew how alcohol could destroy lives. She believed that the state government had to enforce its temperance laws. On June 6, 1900, Nation took matters into her own hands when she walked into a saloon in Kiowa, Kansas, and broke its liquor bottles and mirrors. Then she walked into two other saloons and did the same thing. She rode out of town calling, "Peace on Earth. Good will to men." Eventually she was arrested, but her bold action inspired others to join the prohibition cause.

Reformers were beginning to feel that while passing laws was an important way to bring about change, it was equally important that the government enforce the laws already passed. Progressives began to elect people who would reform the government and enforce laws. They wanted people who represented their ideas instead of those of big business.

NATIONAL POPULISTS

In 1892, farmers formed the National Populist Party. It was strongest in the rural Midwest and South, where many farmers were in debt. They blamed the railroads and other big businesses for their problems. Populist issues included controlling railroads and trusts, helping farmers, and establishing a federal income tax. In 1896, the Populists and Democrats supported the same candidate for president, William Jennings Bryan. After losing that election, the Populist Party disappeared on the national level. The Progressive Party later supported many Populist reforms.

In some places, progressives elected leaders who passed laws to improve the quality of life. Over time, the sewage in the streets was cleaned up, and polluted water was made safe to drink. Buildings were built to be safer. Officials improved fire-prevention rules, and eventually factories improved working conditions. In some cities, progressive leaders worked to reorganize local government so mayors or city councils had less power or were elected more fairly. In some places, corrupt politicians went to jail or lost their power when they were investigated. Others managed to beat the system.

Progressives in New York voted for Theodore Roosevelt, who had begun his political career right out of college when he was elected to the New York State Assembly in 1881. From that point on, Roosevelt was a popular Republican candidate and often won by landslides.

During Roosevelt's time in the New York Assembly, union leader Samuel Gompers took him to see New York City tenements. Soon after, Roosevelt began his long record of reform by trying to improve these housing conditions. He spent his political career working to improve life for all Americans. His progressive ideas changed the way the government operated, first in New York and later at the national level.

During his tenure as New York City police commissioner, he often walked around the city at night to make sure the police were doing their jobs and not taking bribes. As governor of New York from 1898 to 1900, he started many reforms. After President William McKinley chose him as his vice president in 1900, his progression to president was swift. On September 6, 1901, McKinley was shot, and he died a few days later. Roosevelt became president on September 14. Although he promised to continue McKinley's policies, rich businessmen and corrupt politicians worried that Roosevelt would make major changes. They were right.

AN EXCITING LIFE

After his mother and first wife died on the same day, Theodore Roosevelt left New York and politics to work as a cowboy on his cattle ranch in the Dakota Territory. He loved the West and wrote about his experiences. In 1898 during the Spanish-American War, he served in Cuba and led the famed Rough Riders regiment into battle. After the war, Roosevelt became governor of New York.

Roosevelt was a Republican, but because of his progressive beliefs, he became the first president to use the federal government to help people directly. He was guided by his strong sense of what was right and wrong. In a 1903 speech, he promised a "square deal" to veterans, a phrase he later frequently used to mean that he would treat all sides fairly. Roosevelt's ideas about the government's role in helping Americans and regulating businesses had a powerful impact on the country.

Some progressives wanted to change American businesses by having the government take over and run huge corporations, such as railroads and electric companies. Others wanted to break up big companies, like Standard Oil, which controlled whole industries. Roosevelt did not agree with either group. He wanted the government to regulate most big businesses instead.

Roosevelt knew that workers were generally not treated well by large companies. However, he did not believe unions and violent strikes were the answer. In May 1902, coal miners went on strike in eastern Pennsylvania. By fall, the strike was still going, and winter was coming. People needed coal to heat their houses. Roosevelt took action in a way no other president had ever done. He called both sides to the White House and forced them to negotiate. He sent government officials to investigate the problems and helped devise a solution. The miners went back to work with better pay, and people had coal to heat their homes that winter.

That same year, Roosevelt turned his attention toward regulating trusts. He forced a railroad trust, Northern Securities Co., to break into several smaller companies. This was the first of 44 trusts that Roosevelt took action against while he was president. He was labeled a "trust buster," though many of his decisions were simply intended to regulate rather than destroy trusts. He also enforced the Sherman Antitrust Act, the law that allowed the government to regulate trusts. The law had been passed in 1890, but the Supreme Court stopped it from being enforced because of unclear language. The court said trusts did not necessarily interfere with trade between states, but Roosevelt disagreed, and the government began to enforce the act.

While president, Theodore Roosevelt was known for taming the fierce trusts that seemed to control American life.

The American people showed their support for Roosevelt's reforms by electing him president in his own right in 1904. In his second term, he continued to try to improve the lives of most Americans.

In 1906, President Roosevelt read a new novel by muckraker Upton Sinclair called *The Jungle*. This muckraking novel told of the life of workers in the Chicago stockyards and the conditions in meat-processing facilities. Most readers were disgusted by the scenes Sinclair described in his popular book:

> *The whole ham was spoiled ... cut up ... and mixed with half a ton of other meat, ... meat that had tumbled out on the floor, in the dirt and sawdust, where the workers had tramped and spit. ... There would be meat stored in great piles in rooms; and the water from leaky roofs would drip over it and thousands of rats would race about on it.*

President Roosevelt was outraged, and he met with Sinclair to determine whether the descriptions were accurate. When he realized they were, he took action. On June 30, 1906, Roosevelt signed the Pure Food and Drug Act, which forced businesses to improve the safety of their products. The Meat Inspection Act, signed by Roosevelt on the same day, sent inspectors in to stop unhealthful practices in the factories. Soon people felt more confident in what they were eating, and as a result, sales increased. This was important for the progressive movement, because it proved that by creating and enforcing new laws, the government could actually help big business while also protecting workers and consumers.

Roosevelt also sought to preserve the natural resources of the United States. From childhood, Roosevelt had had a special interest in wildlife and nature. As president, he increased the government's role in conservation, the protection of natural resources. He stopped big businesses' uncontrolled use of forests, minerals, and land. He created the U.S. Forest Service and appointed his friend and fellow conservationist Gifford Pinchot as its head. The U.S. Forest Service protected millions of acres of land by establishing national forests, parks, and wildlife refuges.

Roosevelt's "square deal" reforms had made him very popular with the American people. But prior to the 1908 presidential election, he announced that he would not run for president again. Though he knew he could be re-elected if he ran, Roosevelt felt that two terms had been enough. Instead, he supported William Howard Taft, his secretary of war, as the Republican presidential candidate. Though Taft did not want to be president, Roosevelt talked him into becoming the Republican candidate. With the popular Roosevelt backing him, Taft defeated Democratic challenger William Jennings Bryan in the 1908 election.

In 1908, William Howard Taft campaigned for the presidency, and he won with the help of Roosevelt.

Not wanting Taft to feel as if someone were always looking over his shoulder, Roosevelt went on a long vacation to Africa for the first months of Taft's presidency. While away, he heard very little news about what was happening at home. After he returned home, however, he was in for an unpleasant surprise.

35

Conservatives and Progressives

During his 1908 campaign, Taft promised to continue Roosevelt's reforms. Like his predecessor, Taft set his sights on trusts. As president, Taft filed 90 antitrust lawsuits—more than Roosevelt's administration was responsible for. In a 1911 court decision against the American Tobacco Co., for example, this trust was forced to break up into smaller companies.

Progressives also wanted to change the Constitution to allow voters to elect U.S. senators. At the time, U.S. senators were elected by state legislatures, which were often controlled by big business. Because of its rich, sometimes corrupt senators, the U.S. Senate was often called the Millionaire's Club. Many senators resisted the idea of changing the election process because they were worried about losing their power. Finally, in

William Howard Taft, the 27th president of the United States, filed numerous antitrust lawsuits during his presidency.

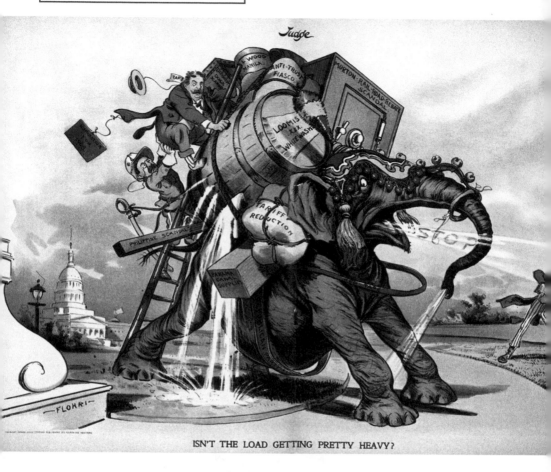

ISN'T THE LOAD GETTING PRETTY HEAVY?

Many conservative Republicans felt the party was suffering because Taft was instituting too many of Roosevelt's progressive reforms.

May 1912, Congress passed the 17th Amendment, which allowed voters to directly elect the senators who represented them.

Several other reforms were passed while Taft was president. The Children's Bureau was started in 1912 to help improve the conditions under which children worked and lived. And in 1913, Taft established the Department of Labor so that workers could have a stronger voice in the government about issues such as their working conditions, hours, and pay.

Another of Taft's reform initiatives was the introduction of an income tax. Progressives supported this idea because they felt the money raised from taxes on the wealthy could be used to help other Americans. In 1909, Congress passed an income-tax amendment to the Constitution, but it took until 1913 before enough states ratified it as the 16th Amendment.

Though he introduced some progressive reforms, Taft was much more conservative than progressive. One of his campaign promises had been to lower tariffs, the taxes on goods coming into the United States. The company importing the goods pays a tariff and then passes that cost along to consumers as part of the price for the goods. Most American companies favored high tariffs because they forced foreign competitors to increase prices. This meant that American-made goods could be sold at a higher price.

When President Taft asked Congress to lower tariffs, progressives, farmers, and many others who wanted lower tariffs were thrilled. They believed that prices would drop. But many Republican leaders who supported big business fought against this proposal. Taft, however, did not defend the lower tariffs, so even though the House of Representatives passed a bill that lowered tariffs, the Senate made 800 changes to the bill.

The final tariff act, known as the Payne-Aldrich Tariff Act, actually changed the tariffs very little. The progressives wanted Taft to take a stand and refuse to sign it because it did so little, but he did sign it. Then he made a speech that made them angry:

> *I am bound to say that I think the Payne Tariff Bill is the best tariff bill that the Republican Party has ever passed. ... This is a substantial achievement in the direction of lower tariffs and downward revisions.*

In signing the act, Taft had let all progressives down and had lost the trust of the progressives within his own party. He was beginning to show his conservative beliefs, which were distinctly different from those of the progressives.

Roosevelt's friend Gifford Pinchot had remained in Taft's government as head of the U.S. Forest Service. Soon, however, Pinchot found that Taft did not support conservation as much as Roosevelt had. In fact, in 1909, some of the land Roosevelt and Pinchot had protected was reopened to use by businesses, and one conservation worker was fired because he wanted Congress to investigate why the protected land had been taken away.

Pinchot was very angry, and he wrote magazine articles and letters to Congress asking for an investigation into the matter. President Taft eventually fired Pinchot, even though he knew it would upset Roosevelt. By then, however, Taft had already fallen out of favor with most progressive Republicans.

In April 1910, Pinchot traveled to Italy to meet with Roosevelt, who was still on vacation. Pinchot told his friend about his problems with Taft and brought many letters from progressive Republicans who hoped Roosevelt would run for president again in 1912. But Roosevelt was not ready to abandon Taft yet. He returned to the United States that June and soon became active in politics again. He wanted reform to continue and made speeches in support of the progressive Republicans who were running for Congress.

On August 31, 1910, Roosevelt made a speech at Osawatomie, Kansas. In his speech, he listed the progressive reforms he wanted, including many he had begun while he was president:

Theodore Roosevelt was a powerful and popular speaker who traveled to every part of the country.

> *We must drive the special interests out of politics. ... I believe in a graduated income tax on big fortunes, and in ... a graduated inheritance tax on big fortunes. ... I believe that the natural resources must be used for the benefit of all our people, and not monopolized for the benefit of the few.*

> *We need ... laws to regulate child labor and work for women, and ... practical training for daily life and work ... We need to enforce better sanitary conditions for our workers. ... I believe in shaping the ends of government to protect property as well as human welfare ... but whenever the alternative must be faced, I am for men and not for property.*

Roosevelt called his ideas the New Nationalism. His call for reform excited progressives while angering and even frightening conservatives and big business.

The growing strength of the progressive movement was evident in the 1910 congressional elections. Though 40 Republicans lost their seats to Democrats, progressive Republicans did not lose any seats. In fact, many new progressive Republican senators were elected, as were many progressive Republican governors. It seemed that Roosevelt's campaigning had made a big impact.

In January 1911, progressives formed the National Progressive Republican League (NPRL). They did

WHERE THE PARTIES STOOD

In 1910, the Democratic Party wanted free trade and lower tariffs, and it did not support the idea of big business controlling the country. The party had the support of farmers in the South and the Great Plains, as well as people in urban areas, where powerful political bosses controlled the votes of immigrants. Some Democrats supported progressive reforms. Before Roosevelt became president, the Republican Party stood for a limited federal government that supported big business. Many Republicans kept these beliefs, which put them at odds with Roosevelt and progressive Republicans who pushed for reform.

not want Taft to be the Republican presidential candidate in 1912. The NPRL asked Roosevelt to join them, but he refused. In June, Roosevelt announced that he was not a candidate for president, nor did he support anyone else.

Robert La Follette, a progressive senator from Wisconsin, announced in September 1911 that he would run for the Republican nomination for president. In October, the NPRL agreed to support him. At the same time, though, some NPRL members asked Roosevelt again to run for president. Roosevelt did not want to take control from La Follette, even though he did not think La Follette could defeat Taft. In fact, he did not think either of them had a chance of being elected president. Still, Roosevelt refused to take sides or to announce he was running himself.

That year, Taft's government began an important antitrust case against Standard Oil Co. One charge

Wisconsin senator Robert La Follette wanted to be the Republican candidate for president in 1912, but many Republican leaders did not feel he was well enough known outside Wisconsin.

was that Standard Oil had broken antitrust laws when it took over another company in 1907. At that time, Roosevelt's government had agreed to the takeover. The new case upset Roosevelt because he felt that he was being accused of being fooled by big business or, worse, of breaking the law. Taft refused to back down on the charges, and the case caused a permanent rift between Taft and Roosevelt.

Roosevelt felt the Standard Oil case was a direct attack on him. Along with his other differences with Taft, Roosevelt no longer felt he could support Taft

ROBERT LA FOLLETTE

Like many progressives, Robert La Follette grew up on a farm. After graduating from college, he practiced law and entered Wisconsin politics as a Republican. From 1885 to 1891, he served in the U.S. House of Representatives. In 1900, he was elected governor of Wisconsin. Under "Fighting Bob" La Follette, Wisconsin passed controls on big businesses and trusts. In 1905, La Follette was elected to the U.S. Senate, where he served until his death in 1945.

again. Since Roosevelt did not think La Follette was a strong candidate, in December 1911, he secretly told some advisers that he might run for president. When La Follette heard this news, he became angry and refused to pull out of the race. Finally, in February 1912, Roosevelt made his candidacy official with his announcement, "My hat is in the ring; the fight is on."

By that time, Taft already had 100 delegates who had promised to vote for him. He was not happy about Roosevelt entering the race. He said:

> *An old and true friend, Theodore Roosevelt … has many charges against me. … I do not want to fight Theodore Roosevelt, but sometimes a man in a corner fights. I am going to fight.*

Roosevelt was on the ballot in most of the 12 states holding primary elections, and he traveled to those states to talk about his record as president and the many reforms he would introduce if he won the presidency again.

La Follette won two of the 12 primaries, while Taft won just one. Roosevelt won the other nine states—most by a landslide. When the primaries were over, Roosevelt had 278 delegates, Taft had 48, and La Follette had 36. Theodore Roosevelt was the clear choice among voters.

In the other 36 states, voters did not play a role in nominating candidates—nor did they select their delegates. In many states, the political leaders, sometimes corrupt politicians, decided which candidate the delegates would support at political meetings or state conventions. In 1912, most Republican leaders supported Taft and his more conservative ideas, so they made sure their state's delegates supported Taft. However, in some states, there were conflicts about whether Taft delegates or Roosevelt delegates would represent the state at the convention.

When the delegate count was finally in, Taft claimed to have enough votes to become the Republican candidate for president. Roosevelt disagreed, for in some states, two delegates were claiming the same delegate seat. Roosevelt contested 254 of Taft's delegates. The Republican National Committee, controlled by Taft supporters, had to decide whose delegates would be able to vote. When the committee's final decision came during the convention, Roosevelt received only 19 of the contested delegates. Taft received the other 235. If Roosevelt had received three more delegates, Taft would not have had enough votes to become the

The vast majority of William Howard Taft's delegates were not won through primary elections.

Republican candidate. Roosevelt angrily accused the Republican National Committee of "political theft in every form."

Taft became the Republican candidate for president. Later he said he had stopped the "dangerous menace" of a third-term presidency. However, he had also ended the Republican Party's role in the progressive movement. Immediately after the Republican Convention, most progressive Republicans joined Theodore Roosevelt in forming a new party—the Progressive Party.

The Race for President

After the Republican National Convention of 1912, Roosevelt declared that the newly created Progressive Party would hold its own national convention in August. He also promised to accept its nomination for president. The new party, officially named the National Progressive Party, had to organize quickly. Roosevelt wanted Progressive candidates to run in every state, so within six weeks, the party had to find candidates to run for office, start up their campaigns, and raise money.

The party received mixed support across the country. In six states, all the state Republican candidates remained Republicans but gave their support to the national Progressive Party candidates. In most states, however, candidates had to choose whether to be a Republican or a Progressive candidate based on whom they supported in the national election. La Follette decided to remain a Republican and not to support the Progressives. He was re-elected as Wisconsin's senator and, like others, remained active in the progressive wing of the Republican Party.

The Progressive Party, nicknamed the Bull Moose Party, shared progressive ideas with Democrats and Republicans.

The Progressive Party hoped the Democrats would have a conservative candidate so the Progressives would be the only party with a reform candidate. No one knew who the Democratic candidate would be until late June 1912, when the Democratic Party held its national convention. When the convention began, James Beauchamp Clark, speaker of the House of Representatives, had the most delegates, but not enough to become the Democratic candidate. For eight days, Democrats debated and voted, but still no candidate had enough votes to win. Finally, after voting 46 times, the Democrats made Woodrow Wilson, the governor of New Jersey, the Democratic candidate for president.

More than 10,000 people came to Chicago for the National Progressive Convention. On the whole, the delegates were young, middle-class, and politically inexperienced. Religion was important

WOODROW WILSON

For 20 years, Woodrow Wilson worked at Princeton University, first as a professor and later as the university's president. In 1910, he was elected governor of New Jersey. In his short time as governor, he instituted direct primaries and put in place other reforms, such as the regulation of public utilities and benefits for workers injured while on the job.

to them, so they often sang hymns. More women came than had ever attended a political convention. Women could not vote in many states, but they still wanted their ideas to be heard. Some women came to the convention on their own, but others were sent as official delegates by their state's Progressive Party.

As governor of New Jersey, Woodrow Wilson made several important progressive changes to the state government.

51

AFRICAN-AMERICANS AND THE PROGRESSIVES

Before the start of the convention, the National Committee of the Progressive Party had to choose between two groups of delegates from Southern states. One group included only white men who did not want any African-Americans to represent their states. The other group had both African-American and white delegates. The committee knew that if the groups with African-American delegates were chosen, the party would not get the votes of Southern white voters, who would continue to support the Democrats. Roosevelt decided to support the white delegates to try to break the hold Democrats had over Southern white voters. African-American delegates, however, did represent some non-Southern states at the convention.

On Monday, August 5, 1912, the convention began. Convention Chairman Albert J. Beverage, a former senator from Indiana, gave the opening speech. He said that neither the Democratic Party nor the Republican Party represented the people any longer. He spoke about the issues the Progressive Party was fighting for:

We battle for the actual rights of man. ... We must try to make the little business big and all business honest, instead of striving to make big business little and yet letting it remain dishonest. ... Votes for women are theirs as a matter of natural right alone; votes for women should be theirs as a matter of political wisdom also.

The next day, an even bigger crowd came to hear Roosevelt speak. The former president gave a long speech that was stopped by applause 145 times. He said, in part:

> *Now, friends, this is my confession of faith. I have made it rather long because I wish you to know just what my deepest convictions are on the great questions of the day, so if you choose to make me your standard-bearer ... you shall make your choice understanding exactly how I feel. ... I believe in a larger use of the governmental power to help remedy industrial wrongs. ... In a larger opportunity for the people themselves directly to participate in government and to control their government agents.*

Even before the Progressive Party convention, Roosevelt spoke to large crowds about the importance of progressive reforms.

> *Surely there never was a fight better worth making than the one in which we are engaged. … I hope we shall win, and I believe that if we can wake the people to what the fight really means we shall win. But, win or lose we shall not falter. … The movement itself will not stop. Our cause is based on the eternal principles of righteousness; and even though we who now lead may for the time fail, in the end the cause itself shall triumph.*

The next day, some newspapers described the speech as "full of hot air." Others said Roosevelt was calling for a revolution.

Progressive leaders at the convention went on to establish the Progressive Party's platform. They arrived at a platform only after many disagreements and compromises, since some Progressives wanted more reforms than others. The final platform contained the ideas from two years earlier that Roosevelt had called the New Nationalism in his speech in Kansas.

While the platform was being finished, Roosevelt was nominated as the Progressive Party candidate for president. Several Progressives gave nominating speeches. One was Denver's reforming Juvenile Court judge, Ben Lindsay, who had left the Democratic Party to join the Progressives. Another was given by social worker and reformer Jane Addams—the first woman to ever give a nominating speech at a national convention.

After these speeches, the platform was read and approved. Even today it stands as the clearest statement of progressive ideas ever written. It included ideas on many kinds of reforms:

> *This country belongs to the people who inhabit it. Its resources, its business, its institutions and its laws should be utilized, maintained, or altered in whatever manner will best promote the general interest. It is time to set the public welfare in the first place.*

Finally, the Progressive convention approved Roosevelt's choice for vice president, California Governor Hiram Johnson. Under Johnson,

As governor of California, Hiram Johnson had passed and enforced many progressive reforms.

California had passed direct democracy reforms and limited the railroads' influence in that state's government.

The Progressive Party had a geographically balanced ticket, with Roosevelt from New York and Johnson from California.

Roosevelt and Johnson stepped onto the stage. This was the first time a candidate had ever attended a convention to accept a party's nomination for president in person.

Roosevelt and Johnson

"For there is neither East nor West,
Border nor Breed nor Birth,
When two strong men stand face to face
Though they come from the ends of the earth."
—Kipling

The presidential campaign of 1912 was now under way. Although President Taft had won the Republican nomination, few people really expected him to win, and he did not campaign very much.

Eugene Debs was the Socialist candidate. He had been a candidate for president before but had not done very well. He was supported by some labor unions and often attacked both Roosevelt and Taft, but he was not considered a real threat to the Progressive Party.

That left the real battle to be waged between Woodrow Wilson and Theodore Roosevelt. Wilson's platform, called New Freedom, stressed three things: lower tariffs, changes to the country's systems of banks and money, and continued trust-busting. He wanted the nation's economy to return to one that encouraged more competition. Wilson felt most other reforms, such as safer workplaces, higher pay for workers, and women's suffrage, should be left to the individual states.

Although the Progressive and Democratic platforms shared some policies, Roosevelt and Wilson were very different candidates. Wilson's manner was more formal than Roosevelt's, who spoke loudly with dramatic flair. However, both focused on the issues, and neither made personal attacks. Wilson did not like campaigning, but he did a lot of it, and many people liked what he had to say. He did not visit as many states as Roosevelt, who traveled to every section of the country. But both candidates spoke to huge crowds in cities and to smaller crowds from the rear of trains. Roosevelt campaigned tirelessly, giving as many as eight speeches a day. By October, both Roosevelt and Wilson were losing their voices.

Huge crowds gathered to see Roosevelt wherever he went.

On October 14, 1912, while Roosevelt was on his way to give a speech in Milwaukee, he was

shot while riding in an open car. He slumped over as bystanders grabbed the shooter. A wounded Roosevelt showed his toughness by refusing to go to the hospital until after he had given his speech. At the beginning of his 80-minute speech, he told his supporters:

> *Friends, I shall ask you to be as quiet as possible. I don't know whether or not you fully understand that I have just been shot; but it takes more than that to kill a Bull Moose.*

After his speech, Roosevelt finally went to the hospital, where doctors decided he was not badly hurt. The bullet had been slowed by the steel case for his glasses and the thick papers of his speech. These items probably saved his life. Although Wilson was leading in the polls, Democrats became fearful that sympathetic voters would support Theodore Roosevelt because he had been shot.

On October 30, 1912, in New York City, Roosevelt gave the last speech of his campaign. The floor shook with the stomping of an enthusiastic crowd of 15,000 supporters, half of whom were women who still could not vote. The crowd's cheers lasted for 43 minutes.

SHOT IN THE CHEST

The man who shot Roosevelt was named John Shrank. He did not want Roosevelt, or any president, to be elected for a third term. Shrank said that a vision of former President McKinley, who had been dead for 12 years, had instructed him to shoot Roosevelt. Later, doctors stated that Shrank was suffering from delusions. He spent the rest of his life in a Wisconsin mental hospital.

The next day, Wilson also spoke to a huge crowd in New York City. Their cheers, however, lasted even longer—62 minutes. This was a sign of how things would go on Election Day, which was only a few days away.

By 7 P.M. on Election Day, November 5, 1912, Roosevelt knew he had lost the election. He telephoned Wilson just before midnight to congratulate him. Wilson had won with 6.3 million votes, or 42 percent of the popular vote. Those votes gave him 435 electoral votes. Roosevelt came in second with 4.1 million votes—27.5 percent of the popular vote—but he received only 88 electoral votes. Taft came in third with 3.5 million votes—23 percent of the popular vote—and only eight electoral votes. Debs surprised many people by doing so well, with 6 percent of the popular vote—901,551 votes.

THE ELECTORAL COLLEGE

Whichever presidential candidate receives the most votes in a state wins the delegates from that state. The meeting of these delegates is called the Electoral College. There they vote for the presidential candidates. In most states, whoever gets the most votes gets all that state's electoral votes. In a close race, it is possible to have the most popular votes spread over the whole country, but not the most electoral votes. This happened in the 2000 presidential election, when Al Gore received the most popular votes, but George W. Bush was elected president because he won the most electoral votes.

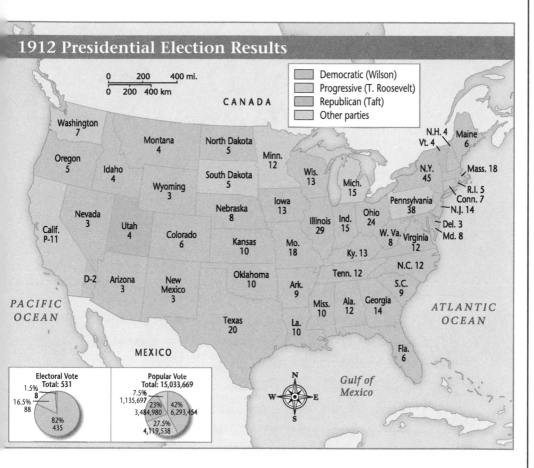

1912 Presidential Election Results

0   200   400 mi.
0   200   400 km

Democratic (Wilson)
Progressive (T. Roosevelt)
Republican (Taft)
Other parties

CANADA

Washington 7
Oregon 5
Idaho 4
Montana 4
Wyoming 3
Nevada 3
Utah 4
Calif. P-11
D-2
Arizona 3
New Mexico 3
Colorado 6
North Dakota 5
South Dakota 5
Nebraska 8
Kansas 10
Oklahoma 10
Texas 20
Minn. 12
Iowa 13
Mo. 18
Ark. 9
La. 10
Wis. 13
Illinois 29
Mich. 15
Ind. 15
Ohio 24
Ky. 13
Tenn. 12
Miss. 10
Ala. 12
Georgia 14
N.H. 4
Vt. 4
Maine 6
N.Y. 45
Mass. 18
R.I. 5
Conn. 7
N.J. 14
Pennsylvania 38
W. Va. 8
Virginia 12
Del. 3
Md. 8
N.C. 12
S.C. 9
Fla. 6

PACIFIC OCEAN
ATLANTIC OCEAN
MEXICO
Gulf of Mexico

N W E S

Electoral Vote
Total: 531
1.5% 8
16.5% 88
82% 435

Popular Vote
Total: 15,033,669
7.5% 1,135,697
23% 3,484,980
42% 6,293,454
27.5% 4,119,538

The Progressive Party lost the election, but as a brand-new party, its members were very proud to have come in second. Party leaders did not disappear, but instead they looked at the results and their goals and moved forward. ◢

The Progressive Party's second-place finish in 1912 was the strongest third-party showing in history.

The Day the Party Died

Chapter

6

The results of the 1912 election showed that most American voters wanted reform. The main reform candidates, Roosevelt and Wilson, had received a combined total of about 70 percent of the popular vote. The Progressives received a bigger percentage of the total vote than any other third party in history. More Progressive Party candidates were elected to local and state offices than candidates from any other third party. Nine Progressives were elected to the House of Representatives, and one became governor. Approximately 260 were elected to state legislatures.

No third party had ever before taken on the Republicans and won. The results revealed both the Progressives' strength in urban areas and their weakness in Southern states and rural areas.

Many Americans believed that the Progressive Party would eventually replace the Republican Party as a permanent political party. Roosevelt promised that the Progressive Party was not through yet:

> *What the Progressive Party has done since ... last June is literally unparalleled in the history of free government. ... The Progressive Party has come to stay. ... So far from being over, the battle is just begun. We will not rest content until every feature of the Progressive program has been put into effect.*

During his campaign, Woodrow Wilson promised to pass progressive legislation.

After the 1912 election, people at all levels remained loyal to the Progressive Party. The party's bold, innovative next step was to establish the Progressive National Service to educate Americans about the need for reform. This service provided books, letters, speeches, and films about the issues, and educated and lobbied politicians at the local, state, and federal level.

In addition, the Progressive Party continued to raise money. The party relied heavily on Roosevelt, whose speeches, letters, and magazine articles kept its name in the public's awareness. Roosevelt also lobbied politicians to pass more reforms. In 1913, Congress, which was controlled by the Democrats, allowed President Wilson to quickly take action on his three most important campaign reforms: lowering tariffs, creating a more independent banking system, and introducing antitrust reforms.

Wilson's 1914 antitrust reforms included the establishment of the Federal Trade Commission (FTC), which investigates unfair trade practices by companies that do business in many states. The Clayton Antitrust Act, which helped control trusts, passed the same year. However, neither action broke up trusts as Wilson had promised during the campaign. Instead, they were closer to Roosevelt's philosophy of the federal government regulating businesses.

In August 1914, the world changed when World War I broke out in Europe. Though the United

MONEY FOR PROGRESSIVES

George W. Perkins was a millionaire who was a board member of several powerful companies. Unlike most millionaires, Perkins supported progressive reforms and the Progressive Party. His donations funded many of the party's activities, and he played an important role in Roosevelt's presidential campaign. Although Perkins was deeply involved with running the party, many important Progressives did not trust him because of his big-business background. Roosevelt remained his champion against those who disagreed with him.

States remained neutral at first, the war had a major effect on Americans' lives. The argument about whether to join the war divided the country, and the loss of trading partners, markets, and goods hurt U.S. businesses.

Over the next few years, Roosevelt publicly disagreed with Wilson's lack of military preparations, although he did not want the country to enter the war at that time. Many members of the Progressive Party did not side with Roosevelt. These included both pacifists, who would not support any war, and party members who wanted the United States to join the war immediately.

In 1914, Roosevelt turned down progressive Republicans from New York who asked him to run as the Republican candidate for governor of their state. He realized, though, that the Progressive Party was not strong enough to win elections on its own. This persuaded him to broaden his support to Republican candidates who agreed to promote

From 1914 to 1917, Americans were divided over whether they should join the war raging in Europe.

the Progressive Party's 1912 platform. Roosevelt's new thinking was so different from his old ideas that it confused many people. Some Progressives felt Roosevelt was betraying them by supporting progressive Republicans, while others felt that the Progressives had to destroy the Republican Party to survive. Still others saw it as a practical decision that put progressive reforms before party loyalty.

During the 1914 congressional campaigns, Roosevelt traveled around the country urging voters to support Progressive Party candidates. He did not encourage Progressives to run against the few Republicans who supported the progressive platform. His popularity enabled him to draw large crowds, but many people left after he spoke without really listening to him. Still, Progressive candidates seemed to be doing well—until President Wilson and the Democratic Congress passed their antitrust reforms. Since the Democratic reforms were very similar to those advocated by the Progressive Party, many voters decided there was no need to support the Progressive Party and instead voted for the Democrats.

The election results shocked the Progressives. Half of their congressional members lost their seats, as did some Democrats. The Republicans made a huge comeback, but they were not able to wrest control of Congress from the Democrats. Many members of the Progressive Party rejoined the Republican Party while continuing to support progressive reforms. Some even lobbied for Roosevelt to be the Republican candidate for president in 1916. They believed, as Roosevelt did, that if the Republicans and Progressives joined forces behind a strong candidate, they could defeat President Wilson.

Roosevelt realized that the Progressive Party would probably disintegrate soon. Wilson and the Democratic-controlled Congress were passing reforms, while Americans became increasingly concerned with the war in Europe and economic hard times. Furthermore, dissension among the Progressive leaders was damaging the effectiveness of the party.

The last battle of the Progressive Party took place in Chicago, Illinois, where the party began. Roosevelt planned the 1916 Progressive National Convention so that it would coincide with the Republican convention. Some politicians wanted a joint candidate, but this was an impossible task. Republican leaders refused to support Roosevelt, and Progressive leaders refused to support anyone else.

Delegates attending the 1916 Republican convention nominated Charles Evans Hughes, a Supreme Court justice who had been a reform governor of New York. Hughes had not been able to take part in politics while he was on the Supreme Court, so most people did not know much about him or his ideas.

Down the street, the Progressive Party began its convention. Few party members understood that Roosevelt was not planning to be the Progressive candidate for president. Roosevelt's goal was to defeat Wilson, and since he felt the Republican and Progressive parties had to unite to do this, he wanted the Progressive Party to support Hughes.

Though Roosevelt's organizers tried to keep the Progressives from nominating him, party members got tired of waiting and nominated him for president because they were sure he would accept. Instead, Roosevelt sent a telegram to the convention in which he refused the nomination. Kansas newspaper editor William Allen White detailed the reaction at the Progressive convention after the telegram was read:

WILSON RUNS AGAIN

In early 1916, all three parties began preparing for the November presidential election. Wilson recognized the desire of most Americans for progressive reforms. He appropriated some of the Progessives' arguments and gained votes by passing reforms. Among them was the Federal Farm Loan Act of 1916, which helped farmers. In June, he once again became the Democratic candidate for president.

> *For a moment there was silence. Then there was a roar of rage. It was the cry of a broken heart such as no convention ever had uttered in this land before. Standing there in the box I had tears in my eyes, I am told. I saw hundreds of men tear the Roosevelt picture or the Roosevelt badge from their coats, and throw it to the floor.*

By refusing to become a candidate, Roosevelt destroyed the Progressive Party. It suddenly had no candidates at either the state or national level. Once the Progressive Party no longer existed, many of its members returned to the Republican Party, while others joined the Democratic Party and supported Wilson. During the presidential campaign that followed, Roosevelt supported Hughes, the Republican candidate, but in the end, the Democrats won re-election. In one of the closest presidential elections in American history, Wilson received 277 electoral votes and Hughes received 254.

The Progressive Party was gone, but it had served its purpose. It had been founded with the purpose of legislating reforms at the federal level. But by 1917, many of the reforms it called for had become law, in part due to the success of Democratic President Wilson. Though the party was dead, progressive ideals continued to shape government policy in the years that followed. ◣

The Party Rises Again and Again

Even though the Republican Party had become more conservative during the life of the Progressive Party, it welcomed back those who had left. In 1917, Hiram Johnson, Roosevelt's Progressive running mate, ran as a Republican and was elected as a senator from California. He remained as one of California's two senators until his death in 1945. Progressives were elected as Republican governors in other states. Several Progressives who were elected to Congress in 1912 but had lost in 1914 later returned to Congress as either Democrats or Republicans.

In his second term, President Wilson continued to adopt reforms advocated by Progressives. Once the United States entered World War I in 1917, Wilson felt it necessary to strengthen the federal

World War I shifted President Wilson's—and the country's—focus away from progressive reforms.

JEANETTE RANKIN

Jeanette Rankin was a progressive reformer who was born on a ranch in Montana in 1880. Like a growing number of women, she went to college and later worked as a social worker. She became involved in the suffrage movement and successfully campaigned for women's suffrage in her home state. In 1916, Rankin ran for a seat in Congress and became the first woman elected to the House of Representatives. One of her first actions was to vote against the United States' entry into World War I.

government and to regulate workers, the workplace, natural resources, and important industries. He had talked about a state's right to regulate business and industry during the 1912 campaign, but the war had changed his attitude, and he instituted many federal regulations in his second term.

Two other reforms that had long been supported by the Progressives were signed into law during Wilson's second term. The demand for a law prohibiting alcoholic drinks had been gaining strength for a number of years. Finally, on December 18, 1917, Congress passed an amendment that outlawed the making, selling, and transporting of alcohol. By 1919, the states had ratified the 18th Amendment, and prohibition became part of the U.S. Constitution. Prohibition, however, did not solve the social problems connected with urban slums, as progressives had expected. Prohibition ended in 1933 when the 21st Amendment was ratified, repealing the 18th.

Another progressive reform, women's suffrage, has had a lasting impact. Roosevelt had been the first presidential candidate to advocate giving women the right to vote. Although by 1918 women had gained the right to vote in 15 states, most states still did not allow them to vote. While suffrage

Women from many walks of life joined marches in support of women's suffrage.

WOMEN'S SUFFRAGE

President Wilson finally asked Congress to pass a suffrage amendment, but the Senate voted it down several times. At last, in June 1919, Congress passed the 19th Amendment, granting women the right to vote, and in August 1920, enough states had ratified it for it to become law. Women all over the country voted in the November 1920 presidential election.

groups continued to lobby both state and national politicians, the tactics of some groups changed. Instead of peaceful marches, they employed a technique no one else had used before: They picketed the White House. They were arrested for obstructing traffic and jailed. Some of the women went on hunger strikes and were treated very badly, but others took their place and continued their fight.

In 1918, some progressive Republicans discussed nominating Roosevelt for president. However, Roosevelt died unexpectedly in 1919, along with the hopes of progressive Republicans. Instead, the Republicans nominated Warren G. Harding, a likable candidate who promised to do whatever the party leaders requested. Reform was not a major issue during the campaign, and in the end, Harding was elected president of the United States.

During the decade that followed, often called the Roaring Twenties, Americans did not take life so seriously. They were not interested in social reforms, regulating trusts, helping farmers, or eliminating government corruption. They just wanted to enjoy life.

Conservatives controlled both the Republican and the Democratic parties, so reformers had little say. But in 1922, several labor unions that wanted new reforms created the Conference for Progressive Political Action (CPPA) to elect progressives to Congress. After a fairly successful campaign, the CPPA asked Senator Robert La Follette to be their candidate for president. He agreed on the condition that they would support the reforms he wanted.

In 1924, the CPPA formed a new Progressive Party with La Follette as its candidate for president. The party platform called for the government to end monopolies, protect people's rights, control the drain of resources, and regulate big business. Since most Americans were not interested in reforms, the party did not do well in the end, and the Republicans won by a landslide. This second Progressive Party, too, disappeared.

President Harding and the two presidents who followed him, Calvin Coolidge and Herbert Hoover, were conservative Republicans. Their administrations did not strictly enforce the progressive reforms passed under Roosevelt, Taft, and Wilson. Big businesses controlled what federal rules were enforced.

In October 1929, the U.S. stock market crashed. The resulting unemployment and bank failures left many Americans desperate for help. Because people did not have money to spend, businesses could not sell their goods or services, and many had to close. The Great Depression followed as business slowed so much that millions of people became unemployed and could not find new jobs.

Although La Follette was a very important progressive, he had never joined the original 1912 National Progressive Party. Yet he had been the second Progressive Party's presidential candidate in 1924. When he died in 1925, his oldest son, Robert La Follette Jr., was elected to take his place in the Senate. At 30 years old, Robert Junior became the youngest senator in nearly 100 years. In 1934, he and his brother, Philip, left the Republican Party to form the Progressive Party of Wisconsin. Robert Junior was immediately re-elected Wisconsin's senator, and Philip was elected the state's governor. Some members of the party were elected to the House of Representatives. This Progressive Party, however, never spread beyond Wisconsin, and it dissolved in 1946.

In 1932, Franklin Delano Roosevelt, a Democrat and distant cousin of Teddy Roosevelt, was elected president. His programs, collectively known as the New Deal, sought to bring the nation out of the Depression. Among his reforms were progressive issues, such as conservation and helping the unemployed. Some past leaders of the Progressive Party joined FDR's government, though others refused because they did not think his reforms went far enough.

FDR went on to become the only president to be elected four times. During his four terms in office, he had three vice presidents. The vice president during FDR's third term was Henry Wallace, who had previously been in charge of the government's farm programs as secretary of agriculture. He was a very politically active vice president, but many in Congress, especially the powerful Southern

For many years, Robert La Follette Jr. was a leader of Wisconsin's Progressive Party, but he returned to the Republican Party in 1946.

77

Democrats who supported segregation, did not like his ideas, especially his ideas about civil rights. Wallace had said:

President Franklin D. Roosevelt (left) spoke about his New Deal programs alongside Secretary of Agriculture Henry A. Wallace.

In a political, educational, and economic sense there must be no inferior races. ... The future must bring equal wages for equal work regardless of sex or race.

As a result, conservative Democrats worked against Wallace, and in 1944, Senator Harry S. Truman of Missouri replaced him as Roosevelt's vice president. Wallace continued to work in the government until Truman, who became president when Roosevelt died, forced Wallace to leave his job in 1948.

That same year, an entirely new Progressive Party was created. It advocated reforms such as more rights for minorities, government price controls, and increased government regulation of big business. This Progressive Party nominated Henry Wallace for president. The Communist Party supported Wallace as well, but since many Americans feared Communists, its support damaged Wallace's position, and in the end, he received only 1 million votes.

This Progressive Party dissolved in 1952, when Wallace disagreed with the party's other leaders over the Korean War. No Progressive Party candidate has run for president since. ◣

Much Good Came of It

Theodore Roosevelt said of the Progressive Party: "Much good came, even though we failed." Little did he know how progressive ideas would ultimately change American life. The party's ideas, for example, would become the basis for the country's welfare system, in which the government takes the responsibility to care for its people, especially the poor and powerless.

Many politicians of today support progressive reforms. They might, like Representative Bernie Sanders of Vermont, call themselves Independents who do not belong to either political party. Others, like Democrat Howard Dean, promote progressive ideals from inside a major party. Often pressure groups form to lobby politicians for a specific progressive reform, such as mine safety, help for the homeless, or conservation.

The process of voting has changed dramatically since the election of 1912.

PROGRESSIVES AND STATE GOVERNMENTS

While Theodore Roosevelt implemented reform on the national level, progressives also worked to reform state governments. In some states, progressives wanted direct democracy reforms that would give voters more say in the government. These often included three reforms—the initiative, the referendum, and the recall. The initiative enables voters to propose a law, which the legislature must then vote on. The referendum allows citizens to vote on whether they want a bill to become a law. Finally, the recall allows voters to remove elected officials from their jobs before their terms are over. By 1912, 12 states, all west of the Mississippi River, had initiative and referendum, and seven had recall.

Cleansing the government of corrupt politicians was a critical demand of the Progressive Party. Members felt that corrupt interests controlled both political parties and the government in general. Some Americans feel that this is still true. They believe that both the Democrats and Republicans ignore the interests of Americans while responding to the demands of big businesses, unions, and pressure groups.

The Progressives felt that if there was more direct democracy, then corruption would have less of a chance in the government. In the United States today, we have many of these direct democracy reforms. Many state and local governments allow the initiative, referendum, or recall processes. One California referendum, Proposition 13, passed in 1978 and limited property taxes. Without this income, the government had to cut much of its spending. In 2003, California voters used another of the processes—recall—to remove Governor Grey Davis from office. They elected actor Arnold Schwarzenegger to take his place.

Today, as a result of the 19th Amendment to the U.S. Constitution, millions of women exercise their right to vote, and an increasing number of women are being elected to public office. In 2006, women made up 14 percent of the U.S. Senate, about 15 percent of the House of Representatives, and about 25 percent of important state offices.

The 1912 Progressive Party platform called for the federal government to protect workers. Over the years, many federal regulations were enacted to improve factories and protect the health and safety of workers. New laws were passed to end child labor, define a minimum wage, and limit the workday. They are enforced by government agencies, such as the Department of Labor.

Theodore Roosevelt's philosophy of regulating businesses is a more common government response today than breaking them up. Government agencies like the Federal Trade Commission have been designed to protect consumers, help businesses, and enforce regulations.

Conservation issues were always important to progressives, and especially to Roosevelt. He placed millions of acres of land under federal protection and stopped the destruction of forests and wetlands. He established the National Forest

83

Service to make sure these lands were protected. The progressive idea was that natural resources should be used to supply people's needs, but not be wasted. In contrast, today's conservationists often want to protect certain areas, plants, or animals

Progressive issues such as conservation have become a major issue for today's politicians as pollution increasingly afflicts the environment.

from any use. Today pollution, which was less of a concern in 1912, is a major issue for many politicians. Many Americans are concerned with how to clean up the environment.

Many other progressive goals were achieved later in the 20th century. FDR's programs addressed some of these, such as protecting waterways by building dams and providing retirement income through Social Security. Progressive programs were later passed under President Lyndon Johnson in the 1960s. In 1965, he signed the act creating Medicare, which gave older and disabled Americans health care insurance from the federal government.

The Progressives worked to make life in the United States safer and more democratic. They saw that America's change to an urban and industrial society had not been a positive one for everyone, but they went beyond just identifying the problems —they did something. They were not successful in making all the changes they wanted, but their ideas were so important that Democrats and some Republicans passed progressive reforms. The attitude of the people who supported Theodore Roosevelt's presidency and the Progressive Party became part of the American culture, and today, Americans take for granted a government that helps people in need and that regulates powerful businesses. Our life today is very much a product of the Progressive Party's ideals.

Timeline

1889

Jane Addams opens Hull House in Chicago, Illinois.

1890

Jacob Riis publishes *How the Other Half Lives*, which describes the conditions under which the urban poor live and work.

June 6, 1900

Carry Nation destroys saloons in Kansas as a protest against the state's not enforcing temperance laws.

November 1900

President William McKinley is re-elected and Theodore Roosevelt is elected as his vice president.

September 1901

President McKinley is assassinated; Vice President Roosevelt is sworn in as president.

May 12, 1902

Coal miners begin strike for higher pay and an eight-hour workday, but coal mine operators refuse to talk.

October 23, 1902

Coal miners return to work after a settlement increases their pay and grants them a shorter workday.

November 1904

Roosevelt is elected president.

1906

Upton Sinclair publishes *The Jungle*, which describes the living and working conditions of workers in Chicago's meatpacking industry; Robert La Follette is elected governor of Wisconsin.

1909

President William Howard Taft fires Gifford Pinchot as head of the U.S. Forest Service.

August 31, 1910

Roosevelt gives a speech in Osawatomie, Kansas, in which he describes the New Nationalism and spells out his ideas on progressive reforms.

November 1910

Forty Republican congressmen lose their seats in an election, but progressive Republicans keep theirs.

January 1911

The National Progressive Republican League is founded by Republicans unhappy with Taft and the party's conservative leadership.

March 25, 1911

The Triangle Shirtwaist Factory fire kills 146 young women because of the unsafe working conditions in the factory.

September 1911

Senator Robert La Follette announces he is running for the Republican nomination for president.

February 1912

Ex-President Theodore Roosevelt announces he is running for the Republican nomination for president.

June 7, 1912

The Republican National Committee announces that most disputed delegates belong to President Taft.

June 18, 1912

The Republican National Convention begins in Chicago.

June 22, 1912

 The National Republican Convention chooses Taft as the Republican candidate for president while most of Roosevelt's delegates walk out; Roosevelt announces the formation of the National Progressive Party.

August 5, 1912

The Progressive Party National Convention begins in Chicago.

August 7, 1912

The Progressive Party convention accepts a platform; Roosevelt becomes the party's candidate for president.

October 14, 1912

Roosevelt is shot but still manages to make his scheduled speech.

November 5, 1912

Woodrow Wilson is elected president of the United States.

February 3, 1913

The 16th Amendment, creating a graduated income tax, is ratified and becomes part of the Constitution.

August 1914

World War I begins in Europe.

November 1914

Half of the Progressive Party representatives in Congress lose their seats, and Republicans make a comeback.

June 7–10, 1916

The Progressive Party holds its national convention in Chicago and nominates Roosevelt; when Roosevelt refuses the nomination, the delegates walk out of the convention.

November 1916

Wilson is re-elected president; Jeanette Rankin becomes the first woman elected to the House of Representatives.

January 6, 1919

Roosevelt dies in his sleep.

Timeline

August 18, 1920

Enough states ratify the 19th Amendment, and women's suffrage becomes law.

1924

The Conference for Progressive Political Action becomes the Progressive Party and nominates Senator Robert La Follette for president.

November 1924

Republican Warren G. Harding is elected president.

October 29, 1929

The stock market crashes, beginning the Great Depression.

November 1932

Democrat Franklin Delano Roosevelt (FDR) is elected president.

1934

Robert La Follette Jr. and Philip La Follette found the Progressive Party of Wisconsin; Robert is elected senator and Philip is elected governor of Wisconsin.

November 1940

FDR is re-elected president and Henry Wallace is elected his vice president.

November 1944

FDR is re-elected for a fourth term; Harry Truman is elected his vice president.

1946

Progressive Party of Wisconsin dissolves and Robert La Follette, Jr. returns to the Republican Party.

July 23, 1948

The New Progressive Party nominates Wallace for president during the third Progressive Party convention.

1952

The New Progressive Party disappears after Wallace leaves it.

ON THE WEB

For more information on this topic, use FactHound.

1 Go to *www.facthound.com*

2 Type in this book ID: 0756524512

3 Click on the *Fetch It* button. FactHound will find the best Web sites for you.

HISTORIC SITES

Sagamore Hill
20 Sagamore Hill Drive
Oyster Bay, NY 11771
516/922-4788

Theodore Roosevelt's home features a museum and nature trails.

Lower East Side Tenement Museum
108 Orchard St.
New York, NY 10002
212/431-0233

Guided tours focus on life in New York City immigrant tenements.

LOOK FOR MORE BOOKS IN THIS SERIES

Brown v. Board of Education:
The Case for Integration

The Chinese Revolution:
The Triumph of Communism

The Democratic Party:
America's Oldest Party

The Indian Removal Act:
Forced Relocation

The Japanese American Internment:
Civil Liberties Denied

The Republican Party:
The Story of the Grand Old Party

The Scopes Trial:
The Battle Over Teaching Evolution

A complete list of **Snapshots in History** titles is available on our Web site: *www.compasspointbooks.com*

Glossary

antitrust
describes laws that encourage greater competition by controlling trusts, unfair trade practices, and monopolies

compromise
a settlement in which each side gives up part of its demands and agrees to the final product

conservation
the wise use of natural resources to protect them from loss or being used up

direct democracy
citizens participating directly in government decision-making instead of representatives acting on their behalf

income tax
tax based on earned and unearned income after allowable deductions are taken

lobbied
worked to persuade politicians to act or vote in a certain way

monopoly
a situation in which there is only one supplier of a good or service, and therefore that supplier can control the price

nominate
to name someone as a candidate for an award, job, or government position

platform
a statement of the beliefs of a group

political boss
the leader of a political party who controls votes, dictates appointments, and influences government decisions

popular vote
the number of voters who vote for a candidate

pressure group
a group of people with a common interest who try to influence government decision-makers to their way of thinking

ratify
to officially approve

settlement house
a building in an urban neighborhood that provides important social, health, and educational services to the people who live around it

suffrage
the right to vote

tenements
run-down apartment buildings, especially those that are crowded and in a poor part of the city

trust
separate companies that join to limit competition by controlling production and distribution of products and services

Source Notes

Chapter 1

Page 12, line 10: Patricia O'Toole. *When Trumpets Call: Theodore Roosevelt After the White House.* New York: Simon & Schuster, 2005, p. 179.

Page 12, line 23: John Allen Gable. *The Bull Moose Years. Theodore Roosevelt and the Progressive Party.* Port Washington, N.Y.: Kennikat Press Corp. 1978, p. 17.

Page 13, line 8: Ibid., p. 179.

Page 14, line 16: Ibid., p. 3.

Page 15, line 6: Ibid., p. 5.

Page 15, sidebar: "Progressive Party: 1912–1952" *U-S-History.com.* 6 June 2006, www.u-s-history.com/pages/h1755.html

Chapter 2

Page 19, line 1: Jacob Riis. "How the Other Half Lives." *Voices of the American Past: Documents in U.S. History, Volume 2.* Eds. Raymond M. Hyser and J. Chris Arndt. Fort Worth, Tex.: Harcourt Brace College Publishers, 1995, pp. 58–59.

Chapter 3

Page 25, line 1: Hilda Satt Polacheck. "I Came a Stranger: The Story of a Hull-House Girl." *Voices of the American Past: Documents in U.S. History, Volume 2, pp.* 106–108.

Page 31, line 5: Theodore Roosevelt. "In His Own Words: Life of Theodore Roosevelt." *Theodore Roosevelt Association.* 6 June 2006, www.theodoreroosevelt.org/life/quotes.htm

Page 33, line 11: Upton Sinclair. "The Jungle." *Words That Made American History.* 3rd ed. Eds. Richard N. Current, John A. Garraty, and Julius Weinberg. Boston: Little, Brown, and Company, 1978, p. 283.

Chapter 4

Page 40, line 4: William Howard Taft. "Defense of a Higher Tariff." *Mount Holyoke College.* 6 June 2006, www.mtholyoke.edu/acad/intrel/taft1.htm

SOURCE NOTES

Page 42, line 1: Theodore Roosevelt. "The New Nationalism." *Presidential Rhetoric, Historical Speeches.* 6 June 2006, www.presidentialrhetoric.com/historicspeeches/roosevelt_theodore/newnationalism.html

Page 45, line 7: *When Trumpets Call,* p. 147.

Page 45, line 12: Ibid., p. 166.

Page 47, line 2: Ibid., p. 177.

Page 47, line 6: Ibid.

Chapter 5

Page 52, line 8: C. H. Congdon. *Progressive Battle Hymns.* No publication information available, p. 17.

Page 53, line 3: Theodore Roosevelt. "Address by Theodore Roosevelt before the Convention of the National Progressive Party in Chicago, August, 1912." *Social Security Online.* 6 June 2006, www.ssa.gov/history/trspeech.html

Page 54, line 12: *When Trumpets Call,* p. 200.

Page 55, line 5: "Platform of the Progressive Party. August 7, 1912." *PBS.org.* 6 June 2006, www.pbs.org/wgbh/amex/presidents/26_t_roosevelt/psources/ps_trprogress.html

Page 59, line 7: *When Trumpets Call,* p. 218.

Chapter 6

Page 63, line 5: *The Bull Moose Years,* p. 150.

Page 69, line 1: Ibid., p. 247.

Chapter 7

Page 78, line 4: "Henry A. Wallace: 1888–1965." *U-S-History.com.* 6 June 2006, www.u-s-history.com/pages/h1754.html

Chapter 8

Page 80, line 2: *The Bull Moose Years,* p. 150.

SELECT BIBLIOGRAPHY

Chessman, G. Wallace. *Theodore Roosevelt and the Politics of Power*. Boston: Little Brown, 1969.

Gable, John Allen. *The Bull Moose Years: Theodore Roosevelt and the Progressive Party*. Port Washington, N.Y.: Kennikat Press Corp., 1978.

Hofstader, Richard, ed. *The Progressive Movement, 1900–1915*. New York: Simon & Schuster, 1963.

McGerr, Michael. *A Fierce Discontent: The Rise and Fall of the Progressive Movement in America, 1870–1920*. New York: Free Press, 2003.

Mowry, George E. *The Era of Theodore Roosevelt and the Birth of Modern America, 1900–1912*. New York: Harper Row, 1958.

O'Toole, Patricia. *When Trumpets Call: Theodore Roosevelt After the White House*. New York: Simon & Schuster, 2005.

Roosevelt, Theodore. *Letters and Speeches*. New York: Library of America, 2004.

FURTHER READING

Collier, Christopher and James Lincoln Collier. *Progressivism, The Great Depression, and the New Deal, 1901–1941*. New York: Benchmark Books, 2001.

Green, Robert. *Theodore Roosevelt*. Minneapolis: Compass Point Books, 2003.

Jaycox, Faith. *The Progressive Era: Eyewitness History*. New York: Facts on File, 2005.

Kraft, Betsy Harvey. *Theodore Roosevelt: Champion of the American Spirit*. Boston: Clarion Books, 2003.

Stone, Tanya Lee. *The Progressive Era and World War I*. Austin, Tex.: Steck-Vaughn, 2001.

Index

ABOUT THE AUTHOR

Hilarie Staton has written for students and teachers for more than 20 years. One of her favorite pastimes is searching old documents, books, newspapers, and photographs for information on her favorite subject, history. Stanton lives in New York's historic Hudson Valley.

IMAGE CREDITS